POWER WRITERS

AND THE STRUGGLE AGAINST SLAVERY

Celebrating five African writers who came to the East End of London in the Eighteenth Century

* * *

Phillis Wheatley, Ukawsaw Gronniosaw, John Marrant, Olaudah Equiano, Quobna Ottobah Cugoano

Compiled and Edited by
Tower Hamlets African and Caribbean Mental Health Organisation (THACMHO), Black History Committee

First published in Great Britain in 2005
by Hansib Publications Limited
P.O. Box 226, Hertford, Hertfordshire SG14 3WY
and
Tower Hamlets African Caribbean Mental Health Organisation (THACMHO)
c/o Social Action for Health, Brady Centre, 192 Hanbury Street, London E1 5HU

Email: info@hansib-books.com. Website: www.hansib-books.com

ISBN 1 870518 33 X

Cover design by Ruth Reviere

Design and Production by Books of Colour, Hertfordshire, England

Printed and bound in Great Britain

I have been incredibly impressed by the work of THACMHO over the years and I hope to continue working with this vibrant, warm and effective organisation in the future. It gave me pride to mention THACMHO's work in the House of Commons in a speech to parliament. There can be few other organizations that are so committed to breaking down the barriers and stigma associated with mental health. Thank you THACMHO for the work you do often on behalf of people whose voice has been lost in the system.

Oona King, MP for Bethnal Green (1997-2005)

I wholeheartedly lend support to THACMHO in its efforts to support healing through educational and other activities for members. Programmes like THACMHO engage the holistic approach to individuals well-being. Mental stimulation, especially for cultural events enhances self-esteem and promotes personal growth. The organisation thus 'gives back' to those in the community who are most at need. I wish THACMHO all the best and am happy to lend my support.

Professor Helena Woodard, University of Texas

Acknowledgements

We thank our Ancestors for guidance. We also thank Tower Hamlets Library Department, Philip Mermick, Marcia McCleod, Lolita Cumberbatch, Tony Miller, Social Action for Health, the MELLOW campaign and Tower Hamlets Social Services. We at THACMHO, along with our partners, are eternally grateful to the Black History Committee: Harry Cumberbatch, Sidney Millin, Philip Morgan, Beverley Clarke, Sadie Parkes, Jennifer Jones, Ruth Riviere, Jean Hall and Fabian Tompsett. Without their hard work and commitment this book would not have been possible. We have also used large blocks of the original text of the Power Writers' words to give a first-hand account and allow them to say it as it was. We would also like to thank you, the reader, for sharing with us the rediscovery of our history in the UK, and others too numerous to mention for their help with this project.

THACMHO would also like to thank 'Awards for All' for their financial support with this project.

Our symbol, Tabono, is from the Akan people of Ghana. It represents strength, confidence and perseverance. This quality not only gives us direction but is also reflected in our Power Writers, whose contribution must not be forgotten.

Contents

The events that transpired five thousand years ago; five years ago or five minutes ago, have determined what will happen five minutes from now. All history is a current event.

John Henrik Clarke

A people denied their history is a people deprived of their dignity.

Ali A. Mazuvi

As I look at the past history of the Black race, I feel proud of my antecedents, proud of the glorious past, which no amount of hate and prejudice could wipe from histories (sic) pages.

Marcus Garvey

Until the lion learns to write his own history, tales of the lion will continue to glorify the hunter.

African proverb

Preface

IT IS WITH GREAT PLEASURE THAT TOWER HAMLETS AFRICAN and Caribbean Mental Health Organisation is able to produce this publication. This helps to redress some of the imbalances left by the failure to properly acknowledge the African presence in East London. However our Power Writers also have a world-wide significance.

This publication is also part of a 'Health Through History Programme' which enables African and Caribbean people with mental health support needs to be pivotal in this redress. This initiative enhances their own self esteem and feelings of well-being through their work to improve all communities' understanding of the contribution that African people have made.

We hope you enjoy reading Power Writers and that it encourages and inspires you towards further studies.

Sidney Millin
Chairperson, THACMHO

SIDNEY MILLIN is a Zimbabwean-born journalist who came to the United Kingdom in 1995. He joined THACMHO after being diagnosed with manic depression and became Chair of the organisation in 2002.

RUTH RIVIERE was born to West Indian parents who came to England from Dominica to find work. She grew up in East London and was educated mostly in London. After a number of different courses she decided to study Art. Ruth completed a Fine Art degree in 1999 and went on to design and make greeting cards, jewellery and produce art for book covers.

Foreword

AS THE DEVELOPMENT WORKER OF THE TOWER HAMLETS African and Caribbean Mental Health Organisation (THACMHO) I am pleased to give a little background on the organisation and the development of Power Writers as a walk and a publication.

TIIACMIIO is a 'Uscr-lcd' mcntal health organisation which began in 1996. I was appointed as a consultant to find out the mental health needs of the African and Caribbean communities living in the London Borough of Tower Hamlets. A Steering Group made up of African and Caribbean users of mental health services was formed and organised a conference in the same year to find out the community's needs. The group continued to meet to carry out the conference recommendations until 2000 when the group decided to formally establish as a voluntary sector organisation.

Our central aim is to promote the well being of African and African Caribbean Users of mental health services living or working in Tower Hamlets – and to help make the life of their communities a more fulfilling and liberating experience.

In a short time, the organisation has made a significant contribution to the development of local and national debate and policy on mental health services, especially through our 'Health Through History Programme'. We have produced promotional material on mental health, organised educational trips, public meetings, talks and significantly contributed to Tower Hamlets' Black History Month programme over the years.

Our members run a successful Drop-In session once a week. The year 2004 saw us presenting, in partnership with the Museum in Docklands and The National Archives' *Moving Here* Project, a successful conference and launch of the subsequent report – *The Reminiscence Conference on the History of West Indian Seamen who sailed regularly during the 1950s & 60s on the Harrison Shipping Lines to the London West India Docks*. This work has lead to the development of an educational pack for schools in partnership with the Tower Hamlets Professional Development Centre's Humanities Education Centre. It has also stimulated an interest in the island of Barbados to honour the contribution of the Seamen. THACMHO has established a strong network of support from Local Authority departments, trust bodies, voluntary organisations and Black groups.

The World Health Organisation's 1978 Declaration states, "Health is a fundamental human right" and defines health as a "state of complete physical, mental and social well being and not merely the absence of disease or infirmity".

Consultation conference in 1996 which led to the formation of THACMHO

With regards to the above declaration we find an holistic approach to mental health treatment as a sensitive and proper way to plan and deliver mental health services. A holistic system is designed to treat the individual as a complex being in the context of their environment. It also allows clients to be seen as emotional, mental, social and spiritual as well as physical beings.

Any mental health service which overlooks the holistic model of care will not enable its clients to reach their full potential, but only continue to combat illness rather than achieve health.

One of THACMHO's objectives is to provide opportunities for members to develop positive self-awareness and identity. One of the ways we do this is via our *Health Through History Programme*. In June 2001 the Management Committee agreed to set up a sub committee to develop a programme for Black History Month in October. A successful funding application was submitted to the Tower Hamlets African & Caribbean Forum who coordinated the community Black History Month programme that year. We proposed a project in partnership with a local community historian, Fabian Tompsett, to develop a walk focusing on our five Power Writers who had contact within the East London area now called Tower Hamlets during the latter part of the 18th Century. The aim of the walk not only looked at the lives of the five African writers but also redressed the omission of the African presence in the 18th Century from a recently published book entitled *One Thousand Years of Tower Hamlets History*. We felt the oversight needed to be corrected and as a result became more motivated to publish the first edition of *Power Writers* with the full support of Tower Hamlets Libraries, without whom this book would not have been possible.

We attended a 6 week course on public speaking (provided by Tower Hamlets College) which helped us firstly to articulate the biographic histories for the walk and secondly with our presentation skills. We also organised a talk and slide presentation by the historian Dorothy Kuya on 'How the Atlantic Slave Trade made Britain Great', focusing on the Liverpool experience.

Evaluation comments from the events allowed the sub committee to form their recommendation as part of their report to the Management Committee who endorsed the following:

- That the sub committee continue to meet to develop the evaluation comments and the following recommendations.
- Plan a work programme for 2002 and beyond.
- Develop the *Power Writers* Walk and improve the exhibition.
- Develop work with libraries, museums, schools, churches, youth centres and community groups.
- Develop an international educational project around Sierra Leone
- Develop an historical walk on how the City of London became wealthy from the Atlantic Slave Trade.
- Organise a booklet and a slide presentation of The Walk.
- Organise an historical database on books, articles and videos and make them available to students.
- Organise visits to archive departments and places of historical interest.
- Develop a genealogy project to trace some of the African population that lived in East London during the 18th century.
- Research the Whitechapel Mission building to find evidence of the White Raven Tavern (a meeting place for Black Abolitionist in the 18th Century).

The committee has continued to meet and is steadily working to accomplish the recommendations. Meeting Vincent Carretta editor of *Unchained Voices: An anthology of Black Authors in the English Speaking World of the 18th Century* has been very important. The book has been the inspiration for Power Writers and we are proud of his autographed comment "congratulations to THACMHO Black History Committee, fellow toilers in the vineyard." Professor Helena Woodard, lecturer at the University of Texas, USA, who we also met gave us words of encouragement. Much inspiration came from S.I. Martin when we attended one of his London Walks which was an eye opener. This quote sums up what THACMHO is about and especially the work of our *Health Through History Programme*.

Harry Cumberbatch
Development Worker

Introduction

The Sankofa bird

THERE IS AN AFRICAN CONCEPT called Sankofa. This concept is represented by a bird walking forward whilst looking backward. The success of the Tower Hamlets African Caribbean Mental Health Organisation (THACMHO) has been its ability to move forward while remembering to do the very thing that sustained us through difficult times in this country.

Here we are honouring five African writers who we call our Power Writers. They are amongst the founders of Black literature in the English-speaking world. Phillis Wheatley (1753-1784), Ukawsaw Gronniosaw (1710-1772), John Marrant (1755-1791) Olaudah Equiano (1745-1797) and Ottobah Cugoano (1757-1801). All lived in London during the last quarter of the eighteenth century. This was a period of great social change: the French Revolution (1787-1799), the American War of Independence (1775-1783) and in England there was an Abolition Movement supporting the struggle of enslaved Africans fighting for their freedom.

During this period there was a Black presence throughout the British Isles, including Liverpool, Bristol and London. It was estimated that the Black London population was between 10,000-20,000, mainly men made up of domestic servants, sailors and Black Loyalists (Africans who were guaranteed their freedom as British soldiers during the American Revolution). In London there were Black settlements in Marylebone, Covent Garden and the East End specifically Mile End and Ratcliffe.

It was here in London that the first breakthrough in the abolition of slavery came in 1772. This was known as the Somerset Case. The judge, Lord Mansfield, declared that a Boston slave-owner could not force James Somerset, an African, on board a ship bound for the West Indies. The Africans who crowded in the court gallery immediately celebrated. The judge estimated there were 14,000 slaves in England. After his verdict they could not be recaptured if they took their freedom. This news spread like wildfire throughout the British Empire.

Our Power Writers came to London's East End for different reasons:

> There are already a great Number of black Men and Women who have made themselves so troublesome and dangerous to the Families who brought them over [from the colonies to England] as to get themselves discharged; they enter into Societies, and make it their business to corrupt and dissatisfy the Mind of every fresh black Servant that comes to England; first, by getting them christened or married, which they inform them makes them free (tho'it has been adjudged by our most able Lawyers, that neither of these circumstances alter the Master's Property in a Slave).
>
> **Sir John Fielding, Extracts from *Such of the Laws*, 1768**

Phillis Wheatley to get her book published, Ukawsaw Gronniosaw and John Marrant to find friends and join a religious community, and Equiano and Cugoano were active abolitionists who were involved with the Sierra Leone settlement. These writers give an important account of the issues facing African people at this time.

Following the success of the first edition, our booklet has been circulated nationally and internationally. It has been mentioned in the Houses of Parliament and taken up by some Tower Hamlets' schools – where children did the walk themselves during Black History Month 2004. The success and popularity of the walk has been officially recognised by Tower Hamlets Council who wish to incorporate it within their cultural walks programme. Furthermore libraries, community groups and a variety of other organisations in the UK and overseas have placed orders for our first edition.

All this shows how bringing this information to light gives us a means to rediscover areas of our history which have been hidden for far too long. Out of this comes a powerful tool which facilitates personal and community development through awareness of history. This is an important part of the healing process from the trauma of our past. THACMHO has identified that a strong vibrant and caring community is the best form of treatment that we can get. This publication is aimed at restoring lessons from our history so that our community can face the future with greater confidence, supporting individual self-esteem and enjoying a clearer understanding of the issues which face us today.

Power Writers walk celebrating Black History Month 2002

POWER WRITERS WALK

Our walk starts near where Phillis Wheatley went to get her book published in 1773, and proceeds to Petticoat Lane, where Ukawsaw Gronniosaw used to live. Moving along Whitechapel Road, our walk ends with the kind hospitality of the Whitechapel Mission, built on the site of the White Raven Tavern. It was here that London's Black community discussed abolition issues and going 'Back to Africa' in the eighteenth century.

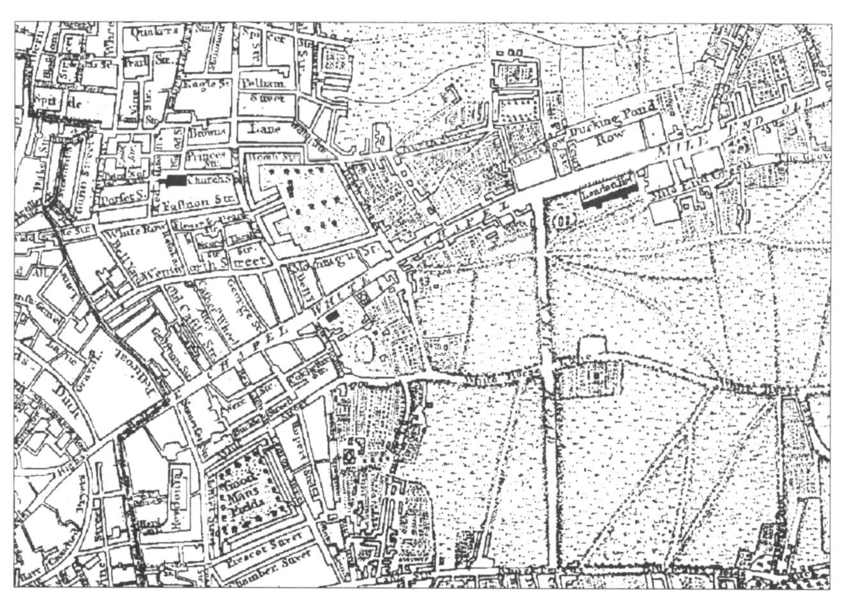

London's East End, 1789

Phillis Wheatley

Portrait of Phillis Wheatley which appeared in Poems of Various Subjects, Religious and Moral, 1773. It has been suggested that this engraving may have been the work of Scipio Moorhead, a young African painter to whom Phillis dedicated one of her poems

PHILLIS WAS A PRECURSOR OF abolitionism. She was born in 1753. Phillis was one of the most well-known poets in America during her day. She was born on the western coast of Africa and kidnapped from the Senegal-Gambia region when she was about seven years old. Her original name was “Fatou”. When she was put on auction at the slave market in 1761 Mrs Susannah Wheatley renamed her. She had been transported to Boston, when she was purchased in 1761 by John Wheatley a prominent tailor, as an attendant to his wife. Phillis was accepted as part of the family and was raised with the Wheatley’s other two children. Because of her poor health, obvious intelligence, and Susannah Wheatley’s fondness for her, Phillis was never trained as a domestic instead she was encouraged by the Wheatley’s to study theology and English, Latin and Greek literature. It is clear that the Christian compassion of the Wheatley family was the nurturing womb in which Phillis’s rare gifts were cultivated. She came to know the Bible well; and three English poets – Milton, Pope and Gray – touched her deeply and exerted a strong influence on her verse.

She was America’s first Black poet. Phillis published her first poem in the Newport Rhode Island Mercury on December 21, 1767, the poem was about the King of England. She became a sensation in Boston when her poem on the death of the Reverend George Whitefield made her famous. Whitefield, the great evangelical preacher who frequently toured New England, happened to be a close friend of Countess Selina of Huntington. Phillis was indeed sensational at a time when it was thought not possible that a black person was able to read and write but she was able to astound her critics.

Unable to get her book of poems published in Boston, Phillis and the Wheatley's turned to London for a publisher with the help of Countess Selina of Huntington. The publisher of her first book was Archibald Bell, based in the East End of London. She was the first African-American to have a book published in 1773.

Her literary gifts, intelligence and piety were a striking example to her English and American audience of the triumph of human capacities

To the University of Cambridge, in New England

While an intrinsic ardor prompts to write,
The muses promise to assist my pen;
T'was not long since I left my native shore
The land of errors, and Eygptian gloom.
Father of mercy, 'twas Thy gracious hand
Brought me in safety from those dark abodes.

Students to you 'tis given to scan the heights
Above, to traverse the ethereal space
And mark the systems of revolving worlds
Still more, ye sons of science ye receive
The blissful news by messengers from heav'n
How Jesus blood for your redemption flows.
See him hands outstretched upon the cross;
Immense compassion in His bosom glows;
He hears revilers, nor resent their scorn:
What matchless mercy in the Son of God!
When the noble human race by sin had fall'n,
He deigned to die that they might rise again
And share within the sublimest skies,
Life without death, and glory without end.

Improve your privileges while they stay,
Ye pupils, and each hour redeem, that bears
Or good or bad report of you to heav'n
Let sin that baneful evil to the soul,
By you be shunned, nor once remit your guard;
Supress the deadly serpent egg.
Ye blooming plants of human race divine,
An Ethiop tells you 'tis your greatest foe;
Its transcient sweetness perdition sinks the soul.

From *Poems on Various Subjects, Religious and Moral,* London 1773, p. 15

over the circumstance of birth. The only hint of injustice found in any of her poems is in the line "Some view our sable race with scornful eye". It would be almost a hundred years before another black writer would drop the mask of convention and write openly about the African-American experience.

Another theme, which runs like a scarlet thread throughout her poetry,

To the PUBLICK.

AS it has been repeatedly ſuggeſted to the Publiſher, by Perſons, who have ſeen the Manuſcript, that Numbers would be ready to ſuſpect they were not really the Writings of PHILLIS, he has procured the following Atteſtation, from the moſt reſpectable Characters in *Boſton*, that none might have the leaſt Ground for diſputing their *Original*.

WE whoſe Names are under-written, do aſſure the World, that the POEMS ſpecified in the following Page,* were (as we verily believe) written by PHILLIS, a young Negro Girl, who was but a few Years ſince, brought an uncultivated Barbarian from *Africa*, and has ever ſince been, and now is, under the Diſadvantage of ſerving as a Slave in a Family in this Town. She has been examined by ſome of the beſt Judges, and is thought qualified to write them.

His Excellency THOMAS HUTCINSON, *Governor*,

The Hon. ANDREW OLIVER, *Lieutenant-Governor*.

The Hon. Thomas Hubbard,
The Hon. John Erving,
The Hon. James Pitts,
The Hon. Harriſon Gray,
The Hon. James Bowdoin,
John Hancock, *Eſq*;
Joſeph Green, *Eſq*;
Richard Carey, *Eſq*;

The Rev. Charles Cheuney, *D. D.*
The Rev. Mather Byles, *D. D.*
The Rev. Ed. Pemberton, *D. D.*
The Rev. Andrew Elliot, *D. D.*
The Rev. Samuel Cooper, *D. D.*
The Rev. Mr. Samuel Mather,
The Rev. Mr. Joon Moorhead,
Mr. John Wheatley, *her Maſter*.

N. B. The original Atteſtation, ſigned by the above Gentlemen, may be ſeen by applying to *Archibald Bell* Bookſeller, No. 8, *Aldgate-Street*.

* The Words "*following Page*," allude to the Contents of the Manuſcript Copy, which are wrote at the Back of the above Atteſtation.

This affidavit was published in the front of the first edition of Phillis Wheatley's book of poems is the salvation message in Christianity – that all men and women, regardless of race or class are in need of salvation.

Phillis Wheatley was emancipated in 1776 and married a free black man in 1778. None of the children she bore lived: she lost all three. She died in child birth with her third child in 1784. (There is speculation on this, researchers said she was sent to an institution by her husband because he could not afford to look after her and the children.) Despite her skills, she was never able to support her family.

Although she died in complete poverty, subsequent generations would pick up where she left off. Phillis Wheatley was the first black writer of consequence in America; and her life was an inspiring example to future generations of African-Americans. In the 1830s abolitionists reprinted her poetry and the powerful idea contained in her deeply moving verse stood against the institution of slavery.

Phillis Wheatley's strongest anti-slavery statement is contained in this letter to the Rev. Samson Occom dated February 11, 1774.

> *Reverend and honoured Sir,*
>
> *I have this day received your obliging kind epistle, and am greatly satisfied with your reasons respecting the negroes, and think highly reasonable what you offer in vindication of their natural rights: Those who invade them cannot be insensible that the divine light is chasing away the thick darkness which broods over the land of Africa; and the chaos which has reigned so long, is converting into beautiful order, and and reveals more and more clearly the glorious dispensation of civil and religious liberty, which are so inseparably united, that there is little or no enjoyment of one without the other: otherwise, perhaps, the Israelites had been less solicitous for their freedom from the slavery; I do not say they would have been contented without it, by no means; for in every human breast God has inplanted a principle, which we call ~It is impatient of oppression, and pants for deliverance; and by the leave of our modern Egyptians I will assert, that the same principle lives in us. God grant deliverance in his own way and time, and get him honour upon all those whose avarice impels them to counternance and help forward the calamities of their fellow creatures. This I desire not for their hurt, but to convince them of the strange absurdity of their conduct, whose words and actions are so diametrically opposite. How well the cry for liberty, and the reverse disposition for the exercise of oppressive power over others agree - I humbly think it does not require the penetration of a philosopher to determine. (First printed in the Connecticut Gazette on March 11, 1774)*

The last parts of Phillis's life were not that nice. Her work fell out of favour. The war left everyone strapped for money. She tried to publish a second book, but there was no response and so it never made it to the market. Finally she had to turn to hard labour. The frail body that had been her weakness all of her life, now had to work in conditions it was unfamiliar with. There is no record of what type of work she did, but the guess is it was very strenuous.

SADIE PARKES: My name is Sadie Parkes. I am of Jamaican parentage. I was born in Paddington, England. My parents moved to the East End of London in the early sixties. I hail from a large family with lots of brothers and sisters so there was never a dull moment. The part of East of London where we lived was Plaistow in a three bed-roomed house. The area was Caucasian dominant, growing up as a child and there was a lot of racial tension in the area and as a family we learnt how to stand up for ourselves and fight our battles and also how to continue on with our lives without being afraid, thanks to my dad.

Ukawsaw Gronniosaw

A NARRATIVE OF THE MOST REMARKABLE PARTICULARS IN THE Life of James Albert Ukawsaw Gronniosaw, an African Prince, as related by Himself, was published in 1772. It was the first Slave Narrative to be published. This became a literary genre as over six thousand of these appeared in the English language. Many of them were brief articles but about one hundred and fifty were published as separate books and pamphlets.

In the first Slave Narratives published between the 1770s and the 1820s the writers generally described themselves as Africans and wrote of their spiritual journeys generally focusing more on the religious redemption they found in Christianity than the social redemption of escaping from slavery. After the publication of The Life of William Grimes, the Runaway Slave in 1824, the Slave Narrative became a major way of exposing the horrors of slavery and campaigning for its abolition.

As Ukawsaw's narrative declares, he was a prince from the city of Bournu, near Lake Chad. He had an unhappy childhood and was considered foolish or insane. He did not get on with his brothers and sisters except his sister Logwy, who was albino. A merchant from the Gold Coast offered to take Ukawsaw with him, promising him the company of his own sons and the opportunity to see houses with wings and to meet White people.

Listening to a reading of Ukawsaw Gronniosaw in Petticoat Lane during the Power Writers Walk, 2002

I began now to entertain a very different idea of the inhabitants of England, than what I had figured to myself before I came amongst them. - Mr. Whitefield received me very friendly, was heartily glad to see me, and directed me to a proper place to board and lodge in Petticoat Lane, till he could think of some way to settle me in, and paid for my lodging, and all my expences. The morning after I came to my new lodging, as I was at breakfast with the gentlewoman of the house, I heard the noise of some looms over our heads: I enquir'd what it was; she told me that a person was weaving silk. I expressed a great desire to see it, and asked if I might: She told me she would go up with me; she was sure I should be very welcome. She was as good as her word, and as soon as we enter'd the room, the person that was weaving look'd about, and smiled upon us, and I loved her from that moment. She ask'd me many questions, and I in return talk'd a great deal to her. I found that she was a member of Mr. Allen's Meeting, and I begun to entertain a good opinion of her, though I was almost afraid to indulge this inclination, least she should prove like all the rest that I had met with at Portsmouth, &c. and which had almost given me a dislike to all white women. But after a short acquaintance I had the happiness to find she was very different, and quite sincere, and I was not without hope that she entertained some esteem for me. We often went together to hear Dr. Gifford, and as I had always a propensity to relieve every object in distress as far as I was able, I used to give to all that complain'd to me; sometimes half a guinea at a time, as I did not understand the real value of it. This good woman took great pains to correct and advise me in that and many other respects.

Gronniosaw then went to Holland but soon wanted to return:

I tarried there a twelvemonth but was not thoroughly contented, I wanted to see my wife; (that is now) and for that reason I wished to return to ENGLAND, I wrote to her once in my absence, but she did not answer my letter; and I must acknowledge if she had, it would have given me a less opinion of her. My Master and Mistress persuaded me much not to leave them and likewise their two Sons who entertained a good opinion of me; and if I had found my Betty married on my arrival in ENGLAND, I should have returned to them again immediately.

My Lady purposed my marrying her maid; she was an agreeable young woman, had saved a great deal of money, but I could not fancy her, though she was willing to accept of me, but I told her my inclinations were engaged in ENGLAND, and I could think of no other Person. On my return home, I found my Betty disengaged. She had refused several offers in my absence, and told her sister that, she thought, if ever she married I was to be her husband.

Sometime later Gronniosaw moved with his family to a place near Colchester in Essex. However after a while they underwent more problems:

My dear wife and I were now both unemployed, we could get nothing to do.

This drawing shows a woman weaving in the upper storey of a traditional weaver's cottage in east London. Image reproduction courtesy of Tower Hamlets Local History Library and Archive

After travelling over a thousand miles he eventually arrived at the merchants home town. However, the King there was scared that he was a spy from Bournu and threatened to personally behead him. However when the King met him, scimitar in hand, he burst into tears and said he could not carry out the execution. However, the King was still too scared to send him back to Bournu, and so compromised by having him returned to the merchant to be sold into slavery.

The merchant dithered, even threatening to murder him as an unlucky inconvenience and Gronniosaw was relieved when a Dutch slave trader agreed to buy him.

Throughout the whole narrative Ukawsaw maintains a quiet innocence which at times has unfortunate consequences for those around him. While he was living as a domestic slave in New York, a fellow slave, Old Ned, warned him that the devil would take him to hell if he swore. When he repeated this warning to his White mistress, she asked who had told him this and Old Ned was flogged. However this incident brought him to the attention of Theodorus Frelinghuysen, a revivalist minister, who soon bought him for £50. Frelinghuysen then encouraged his religious education which

The winter prov'd remarkably severe, and we were reduc'd to the greatest distress imaginable.– I was always very shy at asking for any thing; I could never beg; neither did I chuse to make known our wants to my person, for fear of offending, as we were entire strangers; but our last bit of bread was gone, and I was obliged to think of something to do for our support.– I did not mind for myself at all; but to see my dear wife and children in want, pierc'd me to the heart.– I now blamed myself for bringing her from London, as doubtless had we continued there we might have found friends to have kept us from starving. The snow was at this season remarkably deep; so that we could see no prospect of being relieved: In this remarkably melancholy situation, not knowing what step to pursue, I resolved to make my case known to a Gentleman's Gardiner., that lived near us, and entreat him to employ me: but when I came to him my courage failed me, and I was ashamed to make known our real situation.– I endeavoured all I could to prevail on him to set me to work, but to no purpose: he assur'd me it was not in his power: but just when I was about to leave him, he asked me if I would accept of some Carrots? I took them with great thankfulness, and carried them home: he gave me four, they were very large and fine.– We had nothing to make fire with, so consequently we could not boil them: But was glad to have them to eat *raw*. Our youngest child was then an infant; so that my wife was obliged to chew it, and fed her in that manner for several days.– We allowed ourselves but one every day, least they should not last 'till we could get some other supply. I was unwilling to eat at all myself; nor would I take any the last day that we continued in this situation, as I could not bear the thought that my dear wife and children would be in want of every means of support.

Just as the carrots ran out, as if by a miracle a lawyer in Colchester gave him a guinea:

I went immediately and bought some bread and cheese and coal and carried it home. My dear wife was rejoiced to see me return with something to eat. She instantly got up and dressed our Babies, while I made a fire, and first Nobility in the land never made a better meal.– We did not forget to thank the LORD for all his goodness to us.– Soon after this, as the spring came on, Mr Peter Daniel employed me in helping to pull down a house, and rebuilding it. I had then very good work, and full employ: he sent for my wife, and children to Colchester, and provided us with a house where we lived very comfortably – I hope I shall always gratefully acknowledge his kindness to myself and family. I worked at this house for more than a year, till it was finished; and after that I was employed by several successively, and was never so happy as when I had something to do; but perceiving the winter coming on, and work rather slack, I was apprehensive that we should again be in want or become troublesome to our friends.

From A Narrative of the Most Remarkable Particulars in the Life of James Albert Ukawsaw Gronniosaw, as related by Himself, Bath 1772

Peter Daniell (1733-1792) was a trustee and probably a deacon of the Lion Walk Congregational Chapel in Colchester. Both his father and grandfather were active in the church as were subsequent generations. The church still exists as part of the United Reform Church, which still has some documents written by him.

included reading puritan evangelical texts like Bunyan's The Holy War (1682) as well as the bible.

But the Frelinghuysen family was struck with illness. First Theodorus died but he gave Gronniosaw his freedom from his deathbed. Ukawsaw stayed with the Frelinghuysen family for another six years as first the wife and then the five sons died. Friendless, he was threatened with re-enslavement to pay a debt, but was able to get work as a sailor and then enlisted in the army before making his way to England and adopted the name James Albert.

Here Gronniosaw's Narrative provides an account of working class life in eighteenth century England as he recounts some of the problems which he and the wife he met in Petticoat Lane. They had a precarious existence and one winter barely survived as the family, including three children were living on one carrot a day between them.

Their travels took them to Colchester and Norwich before reaching Kidderminster, where his wife found work in a factory. Here he also met up with Benjamin Fawcett, a dissenting minister with links to the Countess of Huntingdon's Connexion. Fawcett helped him find work and no doubt arranged for Hannah More to take down Ukawsaw's Narrative as he dictated it. It was published in Bath, dedicated to the Countess of Selina of Huntingdon, who had her headquarters there.

FABIAN TOMPSETT grew up in nearby Essex but has lived in London's East End for over twenty five years. His interest in Black History dates back to childhood and he has always seen it as an important issue if contemporary society is to outgrow the current Eurocentric constraints. He sees THACMHO's *Health Through History* as a particularly important way of ensuring that the renaissance of Black British History is rooted in the community.

John Marrant

JOHN MARRANT WAS AN AFRICAN, BORN FREE IN NEW YORK IN North America on June 15th 1755. When he was four years old his father died and the family moved from New York to St Augustine, Florida. There he began his education, he was taught to read and write. After about eighteen months, the family moved to Georgia, where he continued his education until he was eleven. Then they moved to Charleston, South Carolina, where it was assumed John would start his apprenticeship.

Before John could begin his apprenticeship he decided that he wanted to become a musician. His mother disapproved and tried to prevent it but to no avail. On finding that her persuasions were fruitless, she agreed he could commence lessons. She found him a teacher who insisted on a payment of about twenty pounds and that John would stay with him for eighteen months.

He learned so fast, not only to play, but to dance also, that in six months he was able to play to the whole school. In the evenings after the scholars were dismissed, he used to resort to the bottom of the garden, where it was customary for some musicians to assemble to play the French horn. Here he improved so rapidly, that in a year he became master of both the violin and the French horn, and was respected by the ladies and gentlemen whose children attended the school, and also by his teacher. He was invited to all balls and assemblies that were held in the town, and was well known by the local people. After he had served his apprenticeship, his teachers tried persuading him to stay with them, and offered him more money not to leave, but he left to visit his mother in the country. He stayed with her for two months.

Mile End, 2003. We have not yet been able to identify the precise location of the building where John Marrant lived

During this time he and a friend entered a hall where the celebrated Methodist, George Whitefield, was preaching. They

~ I was at the siege of CharlesTown, and passed through many dangers. When the town was taken, my old royal benefactor and convert, the king of the Cherokee Indians, riding into the town with General Clinton, saw me, and knew me: He alighted off his horse, and came to me; said he was glad to see me; that his daughter was very happy, and sometimes longed to get out of the body.

~ I was in the engagement with the Dutch off the Dogger Bank, on board the Princess Amelia, of eighty-four guns. We had a great number killed and wounded; the deck was running with blood; six men were killed, and three wounded, stationed at the same gun with me; my head and face were covered with the blood and brains of the slain: I was wounded, but did not fall, till a quarter of an hour before the engagement ended, and was happy in my soul during the whole of it."

~ Being taken ill of my old wounds I was put into the hospital at Plymouth, and had not been there long when the physician gave it as his opinion, that I should not be capable of serving the king again; I was therefore discharged, and came to London, where I lived with a respectable and pious merchant near three years, who was unwilling to part with me. During this time I saw my call to the ministry fuller and clearer; had a feeling concern for the salvation of my countrymen: I carried them constantly in the arms of prayer and faith to the throne of grace, and had continual sorrow in my heart for my brethren, for my kinsmen, according to the flesh. I wrote a letter to my brother, who returned me an answer, in which he prayed some ministers would come and preach to them, and desired me to show it to the minister whom I attended. I used to exercise my gifts on a Monday evening in prayer and exhortation, in Spa-fields chapel, and was approved of, and sent down to Bath; where I was ordained, in Lady Huntingdon's chapel. Her Ladyship having seen the letter from my brother in Nova Scotia, thought Providence called me there: To which place I am now bound, and expect to sail in a few days.

From *A Narrative of the Lord's Wonderful Dealings with John Marrant, a black, now going to preach the Gospel in Nova Scotia*, Spitalfields 1785

had the intention of disrupting the service, but instead John was converted on the spot. Around the time he accepted Jesus as his saviour he fell out with his family. They felt that his behaviour was bizarre and began treating him like he was crazy. He decided to leave home and began wandering around the countryside.

He met a Native American with whom he travelled and worked for a while. Then he went to a Native American settlement and had the chance to meet and convert some members of the Cherokee community. He was respected in many Native American communities and lived with them for a while, spreading the gospel and winning some converts. His missionary encounter created lasting bonds between the black community and the Cherokee people.

By this time the American War of Independence had broken out, and he was press-ganged into the Royal Navy as a musician. John survived several battles and was eventually discharged in London, He tracked down George Whitefield, the preacher who had converted him, and told his remarkable story. Through this friendship he was introduced to Whitefield's patron, Countess Selina of Huntingdon, who encouraged him to preach to the community. While in England he received a letter from his brother in Nova Scotia, Canada, expressing the need for a preacher for the Black Loyalist community there. So he decided to go there as a Methodist minister.

He was ordained at Bath, as a minister in the Countess Selina of Huntingdon's Connexion, and the countess's friends arranged the publication of his story as A Narrative of the Lord's Wonderful Dealings with John Marrant, a black, now going to preach the Gospel in Nova Scotia, (1785). It was published in 17 different editions and was incredibly successful.

Copy of a Letter from the Rev. Mr Marrant, to Lady Huntingdon, dated North America, Nov 24, 1788

"I hope these few lines find your Ladyship in good health, and all them that love the Lord Jesus Christ. I am now getting a little better, thanks be to God, the Father, through our Lord Jesus Christ, for sparing me to see this day. One of the greatest favours we can receive from virtuous human beings, is to find an opportunity of opening our hearts to them; in doing so we communicate to them an account of our afflictions; our friends naturally sympathize with us, and we are glad of their advice, that advice gives us the same refreshing pleasure as a shower of rain does the weary traveler in the desert of Arabia. It is with a view of obtaining such comfort that I write to your Ladyship. These lines informs your Ladyship my reason in doing so. The bill your Ladyship will find enclosed is drawn by me in favour of Mrs. Margaret Neal. The sum of ten pounds sterling, for value received; it I for things I had in the time of my illness, and the Lord blessed the means that was made use of for my body, so that I am able to go about. I can say that it was good for me that I was afflicted, for here I learn the will of God. I hope to go to Liverpool in a few days, to see the people of God, whom I long to see, that the Lord Jesus Christ will be pleased to enable me to go this journey to the glory of God, and to sing of his name in this world, so that I might die in the works of the Gospel. If your Ladyship will be so kind as to accept this bill, it will be the means of setting your unworthy servant on his way to the glorious works in the Gospel of our Lord Jesus Christ. May this meet with your Ladyship's approbation and love. So no more from me at present.
I remain your humble servant, in Christ
John Marrant

Copy of a Letter from Jonathan Allstyne, to the Rev. Mr Marrant, dated Boston, May 23, 1787

"Rev Sir,
I have just left our friend the Rev. Mr William Furmadge, whose strong recommendations in your behalf, assures me that you are a worthy soldier and servant of the great Emanuel, and that your exemplary life and pious working for the spiritual welfare of the flock you now lead towards Zion, becomes the shepherd of Isrol. I am sorry tat I did not meet you in your circular visits, as it would have prevented me from troubling you with this invitation of meeting me at Liverpool, about the latter end of July. I long to converse with you, and to settle means for our correspondence. Should you have occasion for money to travel with, pray apply to some friend, and I will furnish you (when we meet) with the opportunity to repay them. Should you be want of any temporary provision, pray let me know by your answer, and I will sned you a supply. And as I hear that you have a chapel, and that your people are drove to some extremes, you may very probably need some assistance towards its present establishment. Should that be the case, and you will bring along with you an estimate signed by two or three of the most respected of your followers, I will on account of your brethren at home, enable you to carry your plans in full execution, as I am persuaded that you will obey this brotherly invitation. Pray bring along with you a list of your congregation, with the names of those you entrust with the classes. My reason I shall make known when we meet. Let me further exhort you my beloved that as you struggled with the difficulties of this temporal tabernacle, to manfully maintain the banner as becomes the true soldier and servant; so that we may jointly hail and receive the prize of immortal bliss, to our eternal and everlasting joy. Grace be to you, and all of them of whatever denomination that love our Lord, our common father, in sincerity. Amen, Amen, prays your fellow labourer, brother and servant.
Jonathan Allstyne,
P.S. Direct to me at Dr. Pembrook's, State Street Boston.

While travelling he had many adventures, converting many of his fellow passengers on the trip. Upon his arrival in Shelburne he travelled to Birchtown where he established a church in the centre of the Black Loyalist community. He also expanded his preaching to communities surrounding Birchtown like Cape Negro and Jordan River. He had a lot of opposition from the already established religious community, especially the followers of John Wesley. At one point Marrant and his followers were locked out of the Methodist meeting house. John and his followers persisted and were able to hold their services. The dissension between the different Methodist groups continued and the denominations became quite hostile to each other. John believed what he preached and became very emotional while spreading the word of God. This helped him to connect with people and he won many followers.

Copy of a Letter from the Right Honourable the Countess of Huntingdon, to the Rev. Mr John Marrant Minister of the Gospel in the secreting connection, dated South Wales, Oct 25, 1786

"I have received with great pleasure your two letters; my ill state of suffering bad health prevents my writing so exactly as I would desire to do, and begging our Lord's tender mercy to make me the means of strengthening your hands in his work, and comforting your heart, that you may abide faithful unto death. Many must be the tribulations of the diligent in the Lord's service; but faith, true Gospel faith, will cause us to ride out every storm, and sing our great and glorious deliverer's praises for eternity. I have wrote to enquire after that Mr. Brown you mention, and shall order tickets as you desire, and only writ for your further wants, tickers to send what you want. I think a faithful account of the spread of the Gospel in England and Wales, would cause you and your society to rejoice in the Lord abundantly. Remember me in Christian love to all who love the Lord Jesus; and believe me your truly faithful friend, for his sake.
S. Huntingdon

After his time in Shelburne, due to illness and lack of funds, John left Nova Scotia in January 1788 and returned to England. He published and sold his missionary diary - A Journal of the Rev. John Marrant from August 1785 to the 16th March 1790. It was the most extensive published account of Black evangelism and community life in the eighteenth century. For years before his death in 1791, he was a member of the Free and Accepted Lodge of Negro Freemasons, a branch of the international secret fraternity. John gave a sermon to the Lodge in Boston in 1789 on his way back to England; he died within a year of his return. He lived at 69 Mile End Road and 60 Prescott Street. He was buried in a cemetery in Islington. The graveyard has since been built over.

* * *

MARRANT GLOSSARY: **Connexion** – A group of church congregations that shared ministers who went from church to church; **Providence** – A religious concept whereby God was seen as intervening in people's lives as part of some divine plan; **Press Gang** – Recruiting agents for the British Royal Navy who would use force to make their victims join up

BEVERLEY CLARKE was born in Jamaica in 1950 and came to England in 1960. She was educated in Derbyshire and, after leaving college, trained as a nurse before coming to London in 1972. After nursing for 29 years she retired due to ill health in 1994. Following this she lost her confidence which was restored after she joined THACMHO in 1996. She took part in the West Indian Seamen's Reminiscence Conference and gave a short speech and presented Leonard Evelyn with a book. Beverley sits as Secretary on THACMHO's Management Committee. A major part of her recovery and present support is due to the concern and love of her two children.

Olaudah Equiano

NEARLY 300 YEARS ago, while the world slave trade was still at its height, a former slave, living in London, made a striking impact in promoting the anti-slavery (abolitionist) cause by the publication of a book in 1789 entitled The Interesting Narrative of the Life of Olaudah Equiano or Gustavus Vassa the African. This book was an autobiographical account of his life, from his childhood in Africa, slavery in America and the Caribbean (West Indies) and as a free man in London.

Equiano was born in 1745 in a region of Africa that is now Eastern Nigeria. At the age of ten he was kidnapped with his sister by local raiders in search of slaves, and was ultimately sold to slavers bound for the Caribbean.

Slavery in America and the Caribbean

On initial arrival in Barbados, he was transported to a plantation in Virginia (America). In 1757 (aged twelve years), he was purchased by a lieutenant in the Royal Navy as a present for friends in England. It was during this time that he was given the name Gustavus Vassa, by which he would be known for the rest of his life.

Following a brief spell in England, he spent the following eleven years of his life mainly on board merchant and slave ships, travelling frequently between America and the Caribbean islands and became a skilled seaman. By all accounts his personal experiences as a slave were less brutal than the majority of Africans in the Caribbean, the brutality and horrors of which he witnessed at first hand. He learnt to read and write, keep accounts and became a committed Christian.

Freedom and Return to London

In 1766 at the age of 21, Equiano finally managed to buy back his freedom by paying his current master the sum of forty pounds (for which he had been purchased). He raised this money by purchase and trade of various fruit, liquor and provisions that he acquired on his travels throughout America and the Caribbean islands.

On gaining his freedom, Equiano remained in America and the Caribbean for a short while, although his immediate desire was to return to England. Eventually he did in 1768 and soon encountered first hand the stark reality that status as a free black man in this region warranted few advantages from that of a slave.

> We were not many days in the merchant's custody before we were sold after their usual manner, which is this:— On a signal given, (as the beat of a drum), the buyers rush at once into the yard where the slaves are confined, and make choice of that parcel they like best. The noise and clamour with which this is attended, and the eagerness visible in the countenances of the buyers, serve not a little to increase the apprehensions of the terrified Africans, who may well be supposed to consider them as the ministers of that destruction to which they think themselves devoted. In this manner, without scruple, are relations and friends separated, most of them never to see each other again.
>
> I remember in the vessel in which I was brought over, in the men's apartment, there were several brothers, who, in the sale, were sold in different lots; and it was very moving on this occasion to see and hear their cries at parting.
>
> O, ye nominal Christians! Might not an African ask you, learned you this from God? Who says unto you, Do unto all men as you would men should do unto you? Is it not enough that we are torn from our country and friends to toil for your luxury and lust of gain? Must every tender feeling be likewise sacrificed for your avarice? Are the dearest friends and relations, now rendered more dear by their separation from their kindred, still to be parted from each other, ...Why are parents to lose their children, brothers their sisters, or husbands their wives? Surely this is a new refinement in cruelty, which, while it has no advantage to atone for it, thus aggravates distress, and adds fresh horrors even to the wretchedness of slavery.

A Life of Adventure

As a free man, Equiano had many adventures and travelled widely:

- Involved in a shipwreck in the Bahamas Islands in 1767
- Learnt trade as a hairdresser and worked in Pall Mall, London in 1768
- Travelled throughout Europe by sea including Italy, Turkey and Portugal
- Took part in an expedition to the Arctic in 1773
- Became involved in the Committee for the Relief of the Black Poor in London (based in Whitechapel) and a supporter of the anti-slavery (Abolitionist) movement

Appointment to the Sierra Leone Resettlement Project

Equiano's status within the Navy and as a leading black figure in the anti-slavery movement was illustrated by his official appointment by the Royal Navy in November 1786 as Commissary of stores for the Black Poor resettlement project to Sierra Leone in Africa.

However, his appointment was terminated in March 1787, before the expedition itself set sail for Sierra Leone. Equiano's attempts to highlight the divergence from the original remit of the expedition, the mismanagement of allocated funds and ill treatment of the black settlers made him many enemies. This included, Granville Sharp, a leading member of the Abolitionist movement who accused Equiano of inciting animosity between black settlers and white members of the expedition. Equiano made every attempt to publicly defend himself, and by all accounts was still held in good esteem by the Royal Navy despite his dismissal.

Publication of the 'Interesting Narrative..' and Life in England

Equiano's autobiographical account of his life "The Interesting Narrative of the life of Olaudah Equiano or Gustavus Vassa the African" was first published in 1789, and was immediately recognised as an important contribution to the heightened debate on the fate of the African slave in the Caribbean and America and their treatment by the plantation owners. The book later appeared in many editions and he travelled throughout Britain selling copies and making speeches against slavery.

Equiano himself made some attempt to return to Africa; he volunteered to go as a Missionary but was refused, and also applied as an explorer for the Africa Association.

But he spent the remainder of his life in England, and in April 1792 he married a Miss S. Cullen in Soham, Cambridge. There is not a great deal of documentary evidence of the latter years of Equiano's life, but there is some evidence that he had a daughter Ann-Maria Vassa who died aged four years, less than three months after that of Equiano himself in 1797.

Conclusion

Equiano's life by all accounts was a remarkable one. He encountered the dehumanising snare of slavery as a child and by his forceful character and good fortune remained a learned, dignified and respected figure ardently striving to highlight the brutality and inhumanity of the life of the African slave in America and the Caribbean.

To the present day, Equiano's book remains a simple, dignified and graphic account of one of the worst crimes against humanity – slavery. It is a respected commentary on the history of the slave trade and is referenced in academic and literary circles. His public stance against slavery made him a champion of the Abolitionist movement, but also made him many enemies. During his lifetime there were public expressions of doubts as to both his African birth and his authorship of the book itself, and these issues are still being debated to the present day.

JENNIFER JONES was born in London of Caribbean parents and has spent most of her life in the East End of London (Hackney). She has always had an interest in history from her time in secondary school. Jennifer first made contact with THACMHO in October 2002 when she attended one of their Power Writers walks during Black History month and was inspired by the apparent wealth of Black historical significance within her own local community and decided to join the organisation's Black History Committee. She currently lives in Walthamstow with her daughter, Janine, and is an I.T. lecturer.

Ottobah Cugoano

OUR FIFTH POWER WRITER IS USUALLY KNOWN BY THE SHORTER form of his African name Ottobah Cugoano. He was born in the city of Agimaque part of present day Ghana. As a child he was kidnapped in 1770 and sold as a slave to plantation owners in the Caribbean island of Grenada. In 1772 he was purchased by an English merchant and taken to England where he worked as a servant and obtained his freedom

Cugoano became a Christian and took the name John Stewart. He has been credited for writing the first substantial directly abolitionist publication in English by an African. His book *Thoughts and Sentiments on the Evil and Wicked Traffic on the commerce of the human species* was published in London in 1787. In it he argued that slavery and Christianity are incompatible and demolished one by one all the pro-slavery arguments.

It is said that his work has been more than an anti-slavery text for it has lasted the test of time. Many of the issues on returning to Africa, reparations and self help are still relevant today. In his later 1791 edition Cugoano proposed establishing a school for Africans who had not yet had the opportunity or could not afford to learn 'the laws of civilisation and the Christian religion.' Not much is written of his later life. However,

St James, Piccadilly, where Cugoano was baptised

Marika Sherwood states that he apparently died around 1801 and his vision for a school for the African community in London was achieved in 1807.

Cugoano married an English woman and continued being an activist as a member of the Sons of Africa a Black abolitionist organisation. One of the first we are aware of in London. The appendix to his book *Thoughts and Sentiments* included an account of his life experiences which he also published separately and added much weight to his abolitionist stand. It was called *The Narrative of the Enslavement of Ottobah Cugoano a Native of Africa*. We are fortunate that he did so, as it gives us a good insight into the horrors of the Atlantic slave trade from someone who physically experienced it.

Kidnap

"My father was a companion to the chief in that part of the country of Fantee (Agimaque and Assignee) When I was 13 years I was snatched, with about eighteen or twenty more boys and girls, as we were playing in a field. We lived but a few days' journey from the coast where we were kidnapped, some of us attempted, in vain, to run away, but pistols and cutlasses were soon introduced, threatening, that if we offered to stir, we should all lie dead on the spot.

We were soon led out of the way which we knew, and towards evening, as we came in sight of a town, they told us that this great man of theirs lived there, but pretended it was too late to go and see him that night. Next morning there came three other men, whose language differed from ours, and spoke to some of those who watched us all the night.

I asked what I was brought there for, he told me to learn the ways of the browfow, that is, the white-faced people. I saw him take a gun, a piece of cloth, and some lead for me, and then he told me that he must now leave me there, and went off. This made me cry bitterly, but I was soon conducted to a prison, for three days, where I heard the groans and cries of many, and saw some of my fellow-captives. But when a vessel arrived to conduct us away to the ship, it was a most horrible scene; there was nothing to be heard but the rattling of chains, smacking of whips, and the groans and cries of our fellow-men. Some would not stir from the ground, when they were lashed and beat in the most horrible manner. I have forgot the name of this infernal fort."

The Middle Passage

"We were taken in the ship that came for us, to another that was ready to sail from Cape Coast. When we were put into the ship, we saw several black merchants coming on board, but we were all drove into our holes, and not suffered to speak to any of them. In this situation we continued several days in sight of our native land. And when we found ourselves at last taken away, death was more preferable than life; and a plan was concerted amongst us, that we might burn and blow up the ship, and to perish all together in the flames: but we were betrayed by one of our own countrywomen, who slept with some of the headmen of the ship, for it was common for the dirty filthy sailors to take the African women and lie upon their bodies; but the men were chained and pent up in holes.

It was the women and boys which were to burn the ship, with the approbation and groans of the rest; though that was prevented, the discovery was likewise a cruel bloody scene.

But it would be needless to give a description of all the horrible scenes which we saw, and the base treatment which we met with in this dreadful captive situation, as the similar cases of thousands, which suffer by this infernal traffic, are well known. Let it suffice to say that I was thus lost to my dear indulgent parents and relations, and they to me. All my help was cries and tears, and these could not avail, nor suffered long, till one succeeding woe and dread swelled up another. Brought from a state of innocence and freedom, and, in a barbarous and cruel manner, conveyed to a state of horror and slavery, this abandoned situation may be easier conceived than described."

Plantation Life

"Being in this dreadful captivity and horrible slavery, without any hope of deliverance, for about eight or nine months, beholding the most dreadful scenes of misery and cruelty, and seeing my miserable companions often cruelly lashed, and, as it were, cut to pieces, for the most trifling faults; this made me often tremble and weep, but I escaped better than many of them. For eating a piece of sugar-cane, some were cruelly lashed, or struck over the face, to knock their teeth out. Some of the stouter ones, I suppose, often reproved, and grown hardened and stupid with many cruel beatings and lashings, or perhaps faint and pressed with hunger and hard labour, were often committing trespasses of this kind, and when detected, they met with exemplary punishment. Some told me they had their teeth pulled out, to deter others, and to prevent them from eating any cane in future. Thus seeing my miserable companions and countrymen in this pitiful, distressed, and horrible situation, with all the brutish baseness and barbarity attending it, could not but fill my little mind horror and indignation."

Living in England

Cugoano's early experiences in England have similarities with some African Caribbean people who came to London 200 years afterwards:

"After coming to England, and seeing others write and read, I had a strong desire to learn, and getting what assistance I could, I applied myself to learn reading and writing, which soon became my recreation, pleasure, and delight; and when my master perceived that I could write some, he sent me to a proper school for that purpose to learn. Since, I have endeavored to improve my mind in reading, and have sought to get all the intelligence I could, in my situation of life, towards the state of my brethren and countrymen in complexion, and of the miserable situation of those who are barbarously sold into captivity, and unlawfully held in slavery."

He was advised by some of his fellow servants to get himself baptized so that he might not be carried away and sold again, which he did and was registered at St James Church.

Cugoano advocated the abolition of the slave trade and the emancipation of the slaves. "A fleet of ships should be sent to the African coast to prevent any further enslavement. Free labour on the plantations would be more productive than slave labour; trade in goods and produce with Africa could eventually be as lucrative as the trade in people. It is the duty of a man who is enslaved to get out of the hands of the enslaver", he counselled.

Cugoano also wrote concerning the case of the Zong in 1783:
"The vast carnage and murders committed by the British instigators of slavery, is attended with a very shocking, peculiar, and almost unheard of conception, according to the notion of the perpetrators of it; they either consider them as their own property, that they may do with as they please, if in life or death; or that the taking away of the life of a black man is of no more consequence than taking away the life of a beast. A very melancholy instance of this happened about the year 1780, as recorded in the courts of law; a master of a vessel bound to the Western Colonies, selected 132 of the most sickly of the black slaves, and ordered them to be thrown overboard into the sea, in order to recover their value from the insurers, as he had perceived that he was too late to get a good market for them in the West-Indies. On trial, by the counsel of then owners of the vessel against the underwriters, their argument was that the slaves were to be considered the same as horses; and their plea for throwing them in the sea was nothing better than it might be more necessary to throw them overboard to lighten their vessel than goods of greater value, or something to that effect. These poor creatures, it seems, were tied two and two together when they were thrown in the sea, lest some of them might swim a little for the last gasp of air, and, with the animation of their approaching exit, breath[e] their souls away to the gracious father of spirits. Some of the last parcel, when they saw the fate of their companions, made their escape from tying by jumping overboard, and one was saved by means of a rope from some in the ship. The owners of the vessel, I suppose, (inhuman connivers of robbery, slavery, murder and fraud) were rather a little defeated in this by bringing their villainy to light in a court of law; but the inhuman monster of a captain was kept out of the way of justice from getting hold of him. Though such perpetrators of murder and fraud should have been sought after in the British Dan in the East-Indies, to her Beershebah in the West.

(Dan to Beersheba were respectively in the northern and southern extremities of the Holy Land. The phrase means from one end of a political realm to another.)

Economics

"What the wages should be for the labour of freemen, is a question not so easily determined; yet I should think, that it always should be something more than merely victuals and cloaths; and if a man works by the day, he should have the three hundredth part of what might be estimated as sufficient to keep him in necessary cloaths and provisions for a year, and, added to that, such wages of reward as their usefulness might require. Something of this kind should be observed in free countries, and then the price of provisions would be kept at such a rate as the industrious poor could live, without being oppressed and screwed down to work for nothing, bit only barely to live. And were every civilized nation, where they boast liberty, so ordered by its government, that some general and useful employment were provided for every industrious man and woman, in such a manner that none should stand still and be idle, and have to say that they could not get employment, so long as there are barren lands at home and abroad, sufficient to employ thousands and millions of people more than there are. This, in great measure, would prevent thieves and robbers, and the labour of many would soon enrich a nation. But those employed by the general community should only have their maintenance either given or estimated in money, and half the wages of others, which would make them seek out for something else whenever they could, and half a loaf would be better than no bread. The men that were employed in this manner would form an useful militia, and the women would be kept from a state of misery and want, and from following a life of dissolute wickedness. Liberty and freedom, where people may starve from want, can do them little good. We want many rules of civilization in Africa; but in many respects, we may boast of some more essential liberties than any of the civilized nations in Europe enjoy; for the poorest amongst us are never in distress from want, unless some general and universal calamity happen to us."

Sierra Leone

"This prospect of settling a free colony to Great-Britain in a peaceable alliance with the inhabitants of Africa at Sierra Leona, has neither altogether met with the credulous approbation of the African here, nor yet been sought after with any prudent and right plan by the promoters of it. Had a treaty of agreement been first made with the inhabitants of Africa, and the terms and nature of such a settlement fixed upon and its situation and boundary pointed out; then might the Africans, and others here, have embarked with a good prospect of enjoying happiness and prosperity themselves, and have gone with a good hope of being able to render their services, in return, for some advantage to their friends and benefactors of Great-Britain. But as this was not done, and as they were to be hurried away at all events, come of them after what would; and yet, after all, to be delayed in the ships before they were set out from the coast, until many of them had perished with cold, and other disorders, and several of the most intelligent among them are dead, and others that, in all probability, would have been the most useful for them were hindered from going, by means of some disagreeable jealousy of those who were appointed as governors, the great prospect of doing good seems all to be blown away."

Cugoano's Legacy

Cugoano's significance for us today is that he not only left us with a very good understanding of the trauma of the Atlantic Slave Trade but a reminder that the mindset, which under developed Africa, still remains. He was not scared of speaking out and accused the Government of the day of encouraging the Slave trade and wrote "is it not strange to think, that they who ought to be considered as the most learned and civilised people in the world that they should carry on a traffic of the most barbarous cruelty and injustice." He highlighted the many contradictions in setting up the free colony of Sierra Leone for returning Africans and asked the question "How can a Government establish a free colony nearly on the spot, while it supports its forts and garrisons, to ensnare, merchandise, and to carry others into captivity and slavery." The most relevant of his legacies is his call for Reparations to Africans for their enslavement; an issue that dominated the United Nations World conference in Durban, South Africa in 2001, and which remains unresolved.

HARRY CUMBERBATCH is a mental health and Community Work Consultant. He came to England from Barbados in 1964 to work with London Transport as a bus conductor/driver in Tower Hamlets. Married with three grown up daughters and a grandson, his working life is wide and varied but his love of community work took him into the Youth Service where he worked in Newham for many years. In March 2004 he received the Experience Corps Certificate of Merit for outstanding service to the community.

The African Presence in London

Ratcliffe, home to many Africans in London during the eighteenth century

AN IMPORTANT AREA RELATING to the study of the African presence in London is evidence which indicates the existence of an ancient African civilisation in Britain and Ireland long before the Celts and Romans. This has been documented in terms of many geographical place names and accounts in British and Irish folklore.

The records also show that the arrival of the Roman Army into Britain at the beginning of the first century C.E. (Current Era) also brought with it a division of Moors. Important artefacts have been found to support this information, they include a carved wooden spoon of an African head, discovered at Southwark Bridge. This is one of the earliest African connections with London.

By the early sixteenth century C.E. it had become fashionable for some Europeans to acquire Africans to bring back with them from their travels. This was thought to embellish their status as they could be seen to have travelled abroad. Examples include Catherine of Aragon who was noted as landing in Deptford in 1501 with African attendants. In the case of King Henry VII an African trumpeter referred to as John Blanke was employed in Greenwich at his royal court.

This is the period prior to the intrusion of the Atlantic Slave Trade. During

Late eighteenth century illustration of Africans at an Abolitionist meeting

On Monday near 200 Blacks, with their Ladies, had an Entertainment at a Public-houfe in Weftminfter, to celebrate the Triumph which their Brother Somerfet had obtained over Mr. Stuart his Mafter. Lord Mansfield's Health was echoed round the Room; and the Evening was concluded with a Ball. The Tickets for Admittance to this black Affembly were 5s. each.

this time the arrival of another group of Africans is recorded as having taken place. Michael Lok, the son of a London merchant was responsible for overseeing an operation which brought a group of West Africans to London in 1555. The intention was to train them as public relations men and interpreters for trading purposes. This was the beginning of a continuous phase Black presence in London.

Black Loyalists

In 1770 on the eve of the American revolution there were about 350,000 African slaves in North America, mainly in the southern states of Georgia, the Carolinas and Virginia. Although the official ideology of the American Revolution was 'liberty' in practice this did not extend to the African slaves. While some free Africans fought for the revolution, like Crispus Atticus who was one of the twelve martyrs of the Boston Massacre, other enslaved Africans were forced to fight for the revolution as slaves standing in place of their masters.

Billy Waters, black street performer in eighteenth century London

It was in this context that Lord Dunsmore, the royal Governor of Virginia issued his famous proclamation promising freedom to any slave who joined the forces of the crown. This was the first mass emancipation of slaves in North American history. Within a week 300 Black Loyalists had joined Lord Dunsmore's forces, doubling the size of his army. And hundreds more kept on streaming to him. Soon he had 800 Black soldiers organised into the Royal

The oppofitionifts have converted numbers of the *black* poor into zealous *patriots*. They affembled, it feems, in Whitechapel, where they held, what the Indians term a *talk*; the purport of which was, that they had "heard of an intention of introducing the *arbitrary French laws*, with refpect to *black people*, as part of the new French Treaty; and they looked upon the *arts* now practifed to inveigle them out of a land of liberty, with the utmoft jealoufy." In this inftance, as in many others, the lenity of our Government operates to the detriment of the nation. Are we to be told what articles in a treaty fhould be adopted or rejected, by a crew of reptiles, manifeftly only a fingle link in the great chain of exiftence above the *monkey*? Should a footy tribe of Negroes be permitted to arraign, with impunity, the meafures of Government? A few conftables to difperfe their meetings, and a law, prohibiting *blacks* from entering our country, would be the proper mode of treating thofe creatures, whofe intercourfe with the inferior orders of our women, is not lefs a fhocking violation of female delicacy, than difgraceful to the ftate. In France, fhould a Negroe cafually arrive, he is efcorted to a fea-port, and difmiffed the kingdom; and why any debafement in the *breed* of the people fhould not be an object of attention in the legiflature, a man verfed in found policy muft be at a lofs to conceive.

Newspaper article from 18th century London

Ethiopian Regiment. They were given a uniform with a badge saying 'liberty or death'embroidered on the chest over their hearts.

The Virginia Congress was scared by this and quickly issued a declaration that said this offer struck at the foundation of Virginian society and promised the death penalty for any escaping slave. After the Loyalist army was defeated in Norfolk, the army embarked on ships, where smallpox decimated the survivors of the battle. Of 800 Black soldiers 300 survived. In 1779 Sir Henry Clinton expanded Lord Dunsmore's proclamation to include the other colonies on the continent. The American rebels also promised to free the slaves of White Loyalists.

In many ways this was simply an economic war and liberated slaves could be re-enslaved very easily. Many slaves were put to work on plantations growing food for the British. The Royal Ethiopian Regiment was dissolved, and most of the Black soldiers were now in the Black Pioneers. However there was also a commando unit called the Black Brigade, commanded by Colonel Tye, a runaway slave who had joined the British Army even before Lord Dunsmore's proclamation. Created a Colonel by popular acclaim (the British Army did not appoint Black officers at this time) he led guerrilla attacks behind enemy lines focusing on hated American Patriots who had executed Loyalists. He died from his wounds following one of these forays.

As it became clear the British were defeated, the Army started to organise the evacuation. General Carleton said that as the Black Loyalists were free at the time of the Treaty of Paris, they should be evacuated along with the White Loyalists. Freedom loving George Washington was furious, claiming that the former slaves were property which had to be returned to their former owners. One of these was Harry Washington, forty three, a "Stout Fellow . . . formerly the property of George Washington"! His name is to be found in the Book of Negroes, a register of Black Loyalists in New York who were evacuated. In the south the behaviour of the British was less honourable with Black loyalists being sold into slavery to ransom White Loyalists.

The bulk of Black Loyalists went to Nova Scotia, although many others came to London while others became soldiers or sailors, or found their way across the Caribbean.

In 1791 Thomas Peters, a veteran who had been a sergeant in the Royal Ethiopian Regiment, visited London to complain that the Black Loyalists of Nova Scotia had been mistreated, given the worst land and denied effective employment. He secured an agreement for 2,000 Nova Scotian Black Loyalists to be escorted by the Royal Navy to Sierra Leone. When they arrived they effectively re-established the colony but quickly fell foul of the Sierra Leone Company. Originally the colony had been set up as a self-governing colony according to the socialist principles codified by Granville Sharpe. However a group of London philanthropist businessmen had taken over the company and started to extract rents from the settlers. Although these rents were comparatively small, the Black settlers knew that this would allow the London bosses to up the rents once the colony started to prosper thanks to their own labour. A new form of exploitation – no thanks!

JEAN HALL is a graduate in African Studies who is a poet with a background in theatre education and television. She is a member of the Nostalgia Steel Band. In 2003 she attended the Power Writers walking tour and decided to join the THACMHO sub-committee.

Sierra Leone and 'Back to Africa'

FOLLOWING THE ESTABLISHMENT OF SIERRA LEONE, MANY Africans joined the settlement. The original Christian-utopian plan for the colony can be seen as an early experiment in socialism with the settlers electing their own governor. However, corruption in England led to the colony having insufficient supplies to survive the problems they encountered. This was aggravated by their delayed arrival. After a third had died, the settlers quarrelled with their neighbour King Jimmy, who destroyed their town.

When Thomas Peters arrived from Nova Scotia in 1791, they agreed to the transportation of nearly 2,000 Nova Scotian Black Loyalists to Sierra Leone. One of the directors, John Clarkson, went to Nova Scotia to discuss the proposal with the Black community there. He promised the settlers land free of any rent and prospective settlers flocked to Halifax whence fifteen ships transported them to Sierra Leone. These ships were financed by the British government in recognition of their service to the crown. Each settler household was given a certificate granting them land in Sierra Leone.

But the Sierra Leone Company set up by London merchants did not ratify Clarkson's promise of land ownership. Although composed of abolitionists, the directors were also merchants whose aims were not solely charitable. Shareholders invested £235,280 for the establishment of an urban commercial centre – Freetown. The directors decided that settlers would only be tenants.

After several years of discontent the settlers asserted their right to manage the colony themselves in opposition to the companies attempt to charge rent. This quickly led to an open conflict in 1799. The company and a section of the settlers became rival hostile armed camps. The dispute was only resolved when the ship arrived with 550 Jamaican Maroons, who were happy to help the company reassert its control of the settlement. This defeat left the settlers in a very bad position.

When Sierra Leone became a Crown Colony in 1808 Thomas Perronet Thompson was appointed governor. He was disgusted by the system of 'apprenticeship' which he saw as little different from the slavery the directors of the company were so vociferous in opposing. Another group of settlers were veterans of Bussa's Rebellion, Barbados. This slave revolt broke out three days earlier than planned on 14th April 1816 and spread across the whole island. 123 captured rebels were spared execution and transported to Sierra Leone.

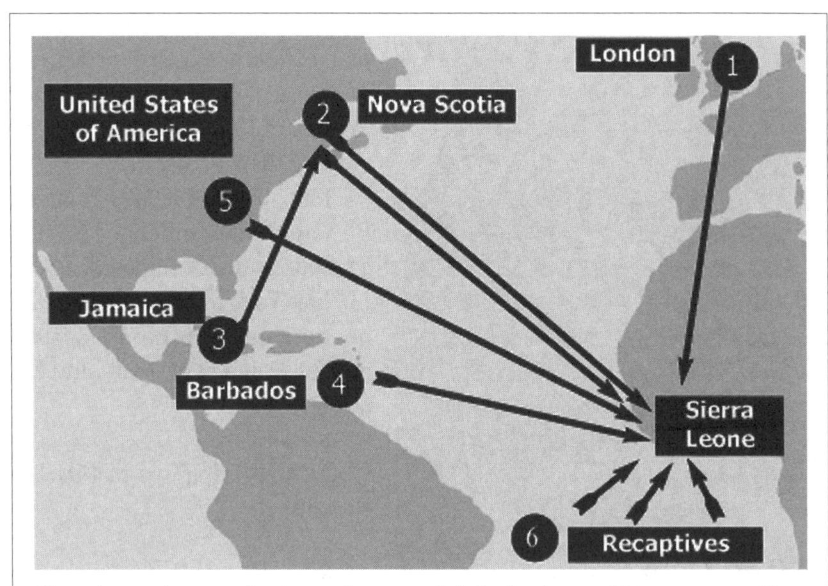

Sierra Leone became the home for several distinct returnee African communities

1. London	1786: The original settlement
2. Nova Scotia	1792: Nearly 2,000 Black Loyalists
3. Jamaica	1796: Maroons were taken to Nova Scotia 1800: The Maroons move on to Sierra Leone
4. Barbados:	1816: Survivors of the Bussa revolt of 1816
5. U.S.A:	1815: Thirty-eight African Americans settle in Sierra Leone arriving in the Elizabeth, a ship captained by Paul Cuffee, a successful African-American ship owner.
6. Recaptives:	1807 on: These were slaves taken by British naval patrols after the government made the slave trade illegal in 1807. Naval patrols off the coast of Africa would remove slaves from slave ships and drop them off at Sierra Leone.

'Back to Africa' in the USA

In the USA the American Colonization Society (ACS) was founded in 1820 but only white people were admitted to membership. Soon with the help of the US Navy and their firearms, the ACS negotiated a treaty for the first US colony in Africa. As with the Sierra Leone colony, the settlers found themselves in conflict with organisation who had founded the settlement. However in this case they succeeded in achieving self-government renaming their settlement Liberia. Despite some influx of African-American settlers following the American Civil War (and 345 Barbadians in 1865), the settlement grew slowly with many people migrating from the African interior.

Despite the moralism of the arguments against slavery, the new colony

Marcus Mosiah Garvey, President General of the Universal Negro Improvement Association

did not accord equal rights to the native Africans as to the African Americans. They were also unable to prevent European powers from eroding their borders.

The noted Pan-Africanist, Edward Blyden emigrated from St Thomas in the Caribbean by way of New York to Liberia where he became a prominent writer, publisher and statesman until his death in 1912.

'Back to Africa' up to the Present

After the First World War repatriation, the return of Africans to Africa, became a major goal of the Universal Negro Improvement Association founded by Marcus Garvey. Garvey left his native Jamaica to organise in the USA, but was soon deported. His movement gathered around the aim of uniting Africans at home and abroad. They left a major impact on the African Diaspora. The desire to return to Africa is central to the Rastafarian movement, and many more people of African descent want the option to go to Africa.

The 'African Diaspora' means the dispersal of African people throughout the world. Part of this has been the forced migration through slavery over the last five hundred years.

The Maroons of Jamaica

WHEN OLIVER CROMWELL ORDERED THE ENGLISH INVASION of Jamaica in 1655 it was part of a Holy War against Catholic Spain. John Milton, the county's leading poet, wrote a *Manifesto* which spoke of Spanish atrocities against the Indians of the Americas. Indeed, in Jamaica the genocide of 60,000 Arawaks had been total by the time the English arrived. The Spanish settlers fled to the Jamaican hills with their slaves to resist the English. However, when they lost hope of regaining their plantations, the Spanish colonists fled to Cuba, leaving their slaves to develop their own communities. These were the first Jamaican Maroons.

The original Maroons were based in the Blue Mountains and were known as the Windward Maroons. In 1690 rebellious slaves from the Parish of Clarendon found a secure retreat in the mountainous country to the north of St Elizabeth at Accompong. Over the next thirty years these former slaves waged a guerilla war against the English settlers, with the support of the slaves still on the plantations. Plundering the plantations of supplies, the rebels also swelled their ranks as more and more slaves joined the rebellion. The planters organized a military force to attack the Clarendon rebels, who had previously been organized in small independent groups. Faced with the determined efforts of the planters to suppress their revolt, the different groups of insurgent slaves banded together and elected Cudjoe as their leader with his brothers Accompong and Johnny supporting him. They successfully resisted the British, and became known as the Windward Maroons.

Cudjoe, leader of the Trelawney Maroons
From History of the Maroons (1803) by R.C. Dallas

Reinforced by a group of Windward Maroons called Cottawoods, and runaway slaves from Madagascar, they grew in power and expertise in guerilla warfare, defeating all the forces thrown against them. The Windward Maroons were also emboldened in the east of Jamaica. They continually harried the British occupations forces becoming a rallying point for any slave who wanted their freedom and pinning down all the regular army forces stationed in Jamaica. The British colonists did not want to mobilize the militia – a force a bit like the territorial army composed of civilians whose normal activity constituted the economic life of the colony. They were scared of how this would damage the economy. Instead in 1733 they formed an irregular unit of rangers commanded by Major James. His troops included Black-shot – Africans loyal to the British, mixed race people called "Mulattos" and Musquito Indians brought to Jamaica specifically to help in the war. As R.C. Dallas explains in his *History of the Maroons*: "The Black-shot and Musquito Indians proved of great service in tracing the haunts of the Maroons and of course Cudjoe's settlements and provisions were successively discovered and destroyed: not however without frequent skirmishes, which though terminating in the defeat of the Maroons, were always attended on the side of the assailants with the greatest loss."

The British had broken Cudjoe's lines of communication with the underground resistance on the plantations of Clarendon. Cudjoe responded by removing his headquarters to Trelawney, establishing Maroon Town. His brother Accompong remained in St Elizabeth in the town which was then named after him. From these bases the maroons continued for several years to raid the plantations, and many fugitive slaves rallied to their cause. Eventually in 1738 the colonists assembled everyone who could bear arms alongside the regular soldiers. However, the most prominent colonists were scared that their combined efforts might fail, thereby encouraging the enslaved Africans to join the maroons in open revolt. They persuaded the governor, Edward Trelawney to offer a peace treaty. Army officers were speedily dispatched to open negotiations, as even the news of peace being offered may have inspired a revolt on the plantations which the colonists had left untended. Colonel Guthrie went to Maroon Town and offered peace. Once they had overcome their initial suspicions, Cudjoe and the maroons accepted the peace terms. They had tired of being in a continual state of war.

The treaty assured the liberty and land rights of the Maroons provided they suppressed any rebels on the island and mobilized behind the governor in the event of foreign invasion. Beside being left to run their own community any conflicts with the colonists were to be dealt with according to the colonial magistrates and that a white superintendent, nominated by the governor, was to live amongst the maroons, and having detailed a line of succession after Cudjoe, the governor reserved the right to appoint further chief commanders. The colonists then moved on to subdue another group of Windward maroons under a chief called Quao. However, they never succeeded in subduing a group of maroons gathered around Nanny who remained beyond their reach in the Blue Mountains.

This peace remained in place until 1795, when the second Maroon war broke out. Although sparked off by an incident when two maroons were flogged by a slave who had previously been captured and returned by them – an unnecessary humiliation. However, R.C. Dallas dismisses this reason saying that "these were persons of no consideration" among the maroons. In his detailed account he suggests that their chief complaint was concerning the superintendent. This was Major John James, son of the commander of the rangers employed against them in the 1730s. "Barefoot, he equalled the speed of the hardiest Maroons over the rocks and precipices, darting on with agility peculiar to himself. He was indefatigable in every pursuit to which the Maroons were accustomed and nothing he pursued escaped him. Hunting the wild boar had been his earliest amusement and employment. (…) Had he born a Maroon, he could not have been better acquainted with their character, disposition and prejudices." (R.C. Dallas) The problem was that Major James was too popular with the Maroons. He had been made Superintendent-General of all the Maroons, with his son given particular responsibility for the Trelawney Maroons. When he started to spend more time away from the Maroon settlement, the Maroons complained, in the hope that he would be obliged to return amongst them. However, the House of Assembly sacked Major James and removed his son from Trelawney, replacing him with Captain Craskell. Craskell failed to obtain the respect of the Maroons. Although they had demands for more land and better treatment from the White people perhaps the restoration of Major James might have resolved the issue.

Looking back at Dallas's account of the Second Maroon War, the defeat of the Maroons seems to mainly stem from the fact that they were not really ready for revolt. Their efforts to gain the support of the Accompong Maroons fell on deaf ears (and indeed the Accompong Maroons do not have a high opinion of the Trelawney Maroons to this day), and the enslaved Africans on the plantations showed little interest in joining a revolt by those who had helped hunt them down so recently. Indeed it is quite possible that whole issue might of passed by without open hostilities were it not for the revolution in nearby Haiti (St Domingo): "the public mind was considerably agitated by the affairs of St Domingo, by the apprehension of the contagion of revolutionary principles spreading to Jamaica, by a currency of vague reports respecting French agency in the island, and by a reluctance to sending troops off the country at so alarming a juncture." Indeed this climate of panic was aggravated by a French prisoner, Jean Josef Moranson, who claimed that 150 French agents – men of colour – had arrived in Jamaica to foment revolution, and that five of these were in Maroon Town. Further the French were planning to land an army of 10,000 African soldiers near Kingston, each armed with two muskets and two broadswords to be distributed amongst the slaves to overthrow the British in Jamaica. This was completely untrue, and indeed it appears that the Maroons knew nothing of the events in St Domingo.

In all events, the Trelawney Maroons were ready for peace, but the British precipitated a war by their over reaction. The Trelawney Maroons were already isolated, the Accompong Maroons and plantation slaves refusing to join them, and the Free Blacks in the militia fighting for the colonial regime. Dallas is at times a bit scathing about the Trelawney Maroons, but even then sums up the situation thus: "When it is recollected that a handful of untrained negroes had, for near five months, defied the whole force of the island, and some of the best troops in his Majesty's service; that many valuable lives had been lost in the contest, while scarcely a rebel had fallen; that many parts of the country had been laid waste; that the enemy who were to be reduced fought differently from every other enemy, could easily evade their assailants, and remove by ways, unknown and inaccessible to the troops from one part of the island to the other; and that they were the descendants of a race of people who had on a similar contest, and by similar warfare, gained their objects, it will not appear surprising that every man who had a stake in the country, every inhabitant of the colony, should feel alarm, and be anxious for the termination of the war."

As all fear of French involvement evaporated the Maroons attempts to sue for peace were gratefully received by the colonists. However refusing their requests that they should settle in Jamaica as free blacks, arrangements were made for the Royal Navy to take them to Nova Scotia. Here many of them were never happily settled, given poor land in a cold climate. They soon successfully petitioned to be taken to Sierra Leone, where they arrived just as another revolt was happening there. They took the side of the British authorities, whose ships had taken them there, and so putting to an end the hopes of the Black Loyalists for a self-managing community. Their descendants live in Sierra Leone to this day.

Robert Wedderburn and Black History

Robert Wedderburn
From the frontispiece of *Horrors of Slavery* (1824)

BLACK HISTORY HAS BEEN USED for instruction and inspiration for centuries. Much of it, of course, was passed down by word of mouth, but here is an extract from Robert Wedderburn's *The Axe Laid to the Root* No. 4 (1817). The text is addressed to Miss Campbell who appears to have been the heir to a sugar estate – she may also have been Wedderburn's half sister by his mother. *The Axe Laid to the Root* was a radical magazine published in London but addressed to the "Planters and negroes of the Island of Jamaica". Wedderburn understood the power structures of his day as a feature of globalisation, linking the struggles of the working classes in England with the struggles of slaves in the Caribbean.

"Chuse ye, as Moses said to the Jews, I have given you time to consider. Have you decided? Yes, I have. My conclusion is this, a mind free from guilt is a heaven on earth. Human nature wants but little, nor that little long. I will trust to the sympathy of nature's universal law, then call your slaves together, let them form the half circle of the new moon, tell them to sit and listen to the voice of truth, say unto them, you were slaves to the cruel Spaniards stolen from your country, and brought here, but Cromwell, the great, who humbled kings at his feet, and brought one to the scaffold, sent a fleet out, whose admiral dared not return without performing something to please his master. Came here and drove the Spaniards out; the slaves, my people, then fled to the woods for refuge, the invaders called them to return to bondage, they refused; they contended for twenty years and upwards; bondage was more terrific than death. At last, a wise and good man appeared from England, and ventured amongst them without a guard, proposed a treaty of peace, agreeable to their own will, which they agreed to. Here you see my origin, and the cause of my freedom, but I have been tempted to purchase you as slaves, by the example of the white men who are sanctioned by the English government."

The Bussa Revolt, Barbados 1816

WHEN BARBADOS WAS GRIPPED BY THE slave revolt of 1816, this was the first outbreak of violent resistance to the Barbados system of slavery for over a hundred years. After the failure of the 1692 revolt, the system of slavery was not static in Barbados. While the White population had remained pretty much constant, the number of Africans had gone up by fifty percent. Although there were no open revolts during this period, slaves used non-violent methods to improve their living conditions. An important element of this self-emancipation was the development of marketing networks. Slaves obtain small bits of land to grow food which could then be sold by the roadside or the streets of Bridgetown. These traders – called hucksters – were harassed by the authorities, but they could not be eliminated as they played a significant role in the economic life of the colony. In 1784 the Court of Quarter Sessions tried to restrict the street traders to a public market called the Shambles. Here the authorities continually tried to exert their control, so that by 1811 the Court of Grand Sessions was informed that the market had become "a public flogging place to the great disgust and annoyance of all those who go there to buy and sell".

According to the abolitionist writer and researcher, William Dickson, slave owners from other islands "sometimes ridicule the slave discipline of Barbados on account of its lenity" and that "the slaves are indulged with liberties which would be thought very perilous in most other islands." However at the beginning of the nineteenth century, the Barbadian assembly proved most resistant to attempts by the Colonial Office to reform the legal restrictions on slaves which for the most part dated back to the 1688 Slave Code. These are factors which contributed to the disaffection and eventual revolt which was led by slaves whose situation was least oppressive. As Hilary Beckles explains: "These plantation officers (drivers, tradesmen and other artisans) were to spearhead the attack upon the planters. In other words, these slaves who were entrusted with authority and status by their masters, were to use it against them. Theoretically, this meant the self-rejection of their roles as 'middle-management', since they were the ones responsible for keeping the field slave productive and subordinated. In association with the four free-coloured men and the few free blacks, these officers were the vanguard of the armed struggle for general emancipation."

When the rebellion erupted on 14 April 1816, it was widespread but short-lived. Within four days the local militia fighting alongside Imperial troops (which included Black soldiers of the First West Indian Regiment) had defeated the revolt, although military operations continued through till July. Although Governor Leith estimated about 120 slaves being killed, another contemporary account puts the figure at "a little short of 1,000". One White militia man was killed and two soldiers from the First West Indian Regiment also died. The revolt had been sparked off three days early "by the intoxication of one of the revolters". The evidence shows that the revolt was to be island wide, and intended to overthrow the whole system of slavery. Following the revolt, those slaves who were not executed were deported first to Nicaragua, but when the Governor there refused to accept them, they were taken to Sierra Leone.

Hilary Beckles' article, 'Barbadian Slaves and their Struggle for Freedom', indicates how the revolutionaries were influenced by an international movement against slavery: "At Bayleys plantation the chief organizers were Bussa, King Wiltshire, Dick Bailey, Johnny the Standard Bearer, and Johnny Cooper. At Simmonds plantation, they were Jackey, John and Nanny Grigg. In addition to these individuals, the politicisation of the field slaves and the general spreading of insurrectionist propaganda were done by three literate, but poor free-coloured men – Cain Davis, Roach and Richard Sarjeant. Davis held meetings with slaves on several plantations, such as River and Bayleys in St Philip and Sturges in St. Thomas. He propagated the view among the salves in these southern and central parishes that local planters were opposing metropolitan efforts to have them freed, and that if they wanted freedom 'they must fight for it'. Sarjeant was also reported to have mobilized slaves in the central parishes using the same kind of information and techniques as Davis. A small number of literate slaves was also reported to have recruited many slaves in a similar manner, stating that they had obtained their information from English newspapers. The most prominent of these literate slaves was Ben James who belonged to Ayshford plantation in St Thomas.

Indeed agitation in London was not simply for the abolition of slavery – trade recession, high bread prices and the demobilization of the army was generating mass unrest on streets of London. A revolutionary group in England started to secretly plan a revolt. Like the Bussa revolt, the revolt was set off prematurely on 2 December 1816, when the drunken son of one of leaders seized a tricolour at a mass meeting in Spa Filed, London and led a crowd to a ransack a gun shop before attempting to storm the Tower of London. Iain McCalman has described some of the people involved in this revolt: "One of the cutlass wielding ringleaders captured on the day proved to be a black American sailor named Richard Simmonds. He claimed under interrogation that several other blacks and mulattos had been involved in the rising. Wedderburn may have been one of these: his friend and patron, George Cannon, seems to have provided the legal advice which enabled Simmonds to escape with a relatively light sentence of transportation, unlike an Irish fellow sailor named Cashman who was executed for joining the mob."

Robert Wedderburn, referred to here, was the son of an enslaved African in Jamaica who had joined the radical political circles in London. In *The Many Headed Hydra*, Peter Linebaugh remarks that: "Bussa's Rebellion and the Spa Field Riots helped Wedderburn to see that the circulation of information had become dangerous to West Indian planters – and hence his decision to publish the *Axe Laid to the Root*, which apparently reached both of its intended audiences, planters and slaves. A merchant warned the Jamaican Assembly about such publications, 'in which were found doctrines destructive of the tranquillity of this island, containing direct incitement to the imitation of the conduct of slaves of St Domingo [Haiti], and loading the proprietors of slaves with every odious epithet.'"

By 1819 Wedderburn was addressing meetings in London which addressed the question "Has a slave an inherent right to slay his master, who refuses him his liberty?" A government spy reported: "In speaking of a Black man who was hung for the murder of a tyrant, he said he entered the Scaffold with great confidence and his manner indicated that his conscience felt no more guilt than Bellingham's or Cashman's." (John Bellingham assassinated the British Prime Minister, Spencer Perceval, in 1812) The international impact of this network of subversives can be shown by the laws passed in South Carolina: in 1820 the planters passed a law against "incendiary publications". In 1822, the importance of Black sailors in the circulation of information was recognised by the Negro Seaman Act which allowed for the imprisonment of any Black sailor for the duration of their ship's stay in the port of Charleston.

From this we can see that the struggle for the abolition of slavery was not so much the product of social reformers agitating for parliamentary reform as a broad movement including an extensive network of Black seamen, plantation slaves, 'coloured' and Black freemen to be found all across the Atlantic, from England to the Caribbean to North America, and Africa itself.

London's Black African History and Today

LONDON'S BLACK HISTORY IS ONE LITTERED WITH TALES OF displacement and tragic misadventure. The evil horrors of the past have clearly left what may appear to be an indelible mark on the people and infrastructure of Britain today. Even though slavery has long been abolished, many of the prejudices of yesterday still remain intact in an advanced form of what is now called "institutional racism".

The success of Britain as a world power has to be mainly credited to colonialism and slavery. African peoples have made immeasurable contributions to the social and economic infrastructure of Britain for literally thousands of years through language, culture, science and religion to name but a few. The enslavement of Africans undeniably benefited capitalist development in Europe and the Americas far more than many are willing to admit. Millions of Africans were enslaved from the sixteenth century right up to the middle of the twentieth century. The vast majority lived and worked in terribly appalling conditions and had to put up with the most extreme forms of oppression as a centrally essential part of their everyday existence.

In spite of these dark and gruesome facts concerning Black History, it is evident that the spirit and resilience of African peoples remained strong. When they had the chance they diverted and amused themselves with various forms of companionship and entertainment. A few took pen to paper and recorded their experiences so that people of the future might begin to understand the appallingly flagrant depth of atrocities that existed then. Even so, it is worth noting that virtually all records of slavery written by slavers and the like reflected the evils practised therein.

There are several distinct differences between Black writers of the past and those of the present. Without doubt writers of the past were concerned with their bondage and their more recent cultural ancestry. Whereas, many writers of the present are more concerned with other social issues relevant to their modernity, such as; crime, music, sex and violence. Other than that, perhaps the main issues of economic, racial and social oppression can ally themselves to the bedrock of the institutional racism which has remained consistent from the past to the present. This effectively means that despite the vast range of differences and the virtual vacuum between the writers of the past and present, there are interesting similarities linking them together: those being the influence of their life experiences in relation to race, its diasporas and the sub-cultures that have developed as a result.

A BRIEF CHRONOLOGY OF LONDON'S BLACK AFRICAN HISTORY

16th Century

1501	John Blanke served Henry VII and Henry VIII
1555	John Lok and 'certain black slaves' arrive from Africa
1593	"Cornelius", first Black person on Parish Register
1596-1601	Elizabeth I proclaims to arrest and expel all "Negroes and Blackamoors" from her kingdom in response to growing Black population in London

18th Century

1700s	Racial discrimination reduces the limited number of freed slaves to begging
1750-1760s	General consensus that Black people were lower than animals. An increased resistance to slavery from across section of Britons Notable Black activists begin to emerge, Ottobah Cugoano, Olaudah Equiano and Ignatius Sancho
1770s	A sub-underclass of Black poor develops in various parts of London. Many of them were freed slaves with no opportunities. The increase of 'Black loyalists' from America exacerbates these problems. The Poor Law did not accommodate 'foreigners' at that time
1787	The resettlement of Black Londoners to Sierra Leone was proposed by a Special Committee for the Relief of the Black Poor
1789	The Interesting Narrative of the Life of Olaudah Equiano or Gustavus Vassa the African published
1792-1815	Industrial capitalism causes decline in slave trade and further racist issues, such as scientific racism, due to intolerance. Many of the remaining Black community gradually absorbed into the white population as immigration

19th Century

1807	Slave trade made illegal in British Empire
1834	Abolition of slavery by Parliament throughout the British Empire. Compensation paid to slave owners while slaves must work for another seven years "apprenticeship"
1880	New shipping lines with African and Caribbean sailors bring a resurgence of Black dockland communities around Britain

20th Century

WWI	Further growth in Black communities with arrival of ex-servicemen and students from Africa and Caribbean
WWII	Many rejoin services and experience new forms of racism
1948	SS Empire Windrush brings 492 Caribbean immigrants to London
1950-1960s	Invitation from British Government for African-Caribbeans to fill labour requirements in service industries
1962	Commonwealth Immigrants Act restricts entry to Britain. Increased racial intolerance causes further divisions within society and subsequently a new underclass of Black poor arises. This trend continues until the late 1980s
1981-84	Inner city riots occur across Britain, necessitating social reform
1987	The British public elect four new Black Members of Parliament
1991-1997	London's Black Population increases to over ½ million in 1991 census report, the majority being British born. An increase in the number of Black MPs to six (1992) and then nine (1997)

Changes in White British attitudes towards Black people have been far more forced than voluntary which may have further institutionalised racism to a greater extent than it previously had been – this most especially when we consider the fact that the foundations of the British economy were centred on colonialism and slavery. Adding to this, Abolition served a crucial economic purpose. A lot of money was saved through the non-provision of clothing, food, shelter and other everyday social benefits etc. Knowing this, slavers (or ex-slavers) and their associates were able to make even more vast amounts of money through rent, taxes, welfare and the supply of provisions. Furthermore, monies paid by the British government as compensation for Abolition was retained by the slavers with little if any being redistributed to the slaves themselves. Capitalism was further safeguarded by government censuses and official 'race categorisations'. None of which existed before the 'Black' or 'Negro' came to their so-called knowledge. This knowledge, rationalised through a subjective understanding of science and reason justified and formalised many of the divisions that have arisen within our world society over the past five hundred years.

The engagement of Black professionals within government and business institutions has failed to stem the practice of social indifference and rough justice. Sadly many of us (or them!) are seen to be integrated into a system that is inherently corrupt.

The world at present is wrought with a multitude of internal conflicts where earth culture and human identity seem to play little or no real part. Our everyday concept of knowledge is based on material factors and life is merely used to reinforce that false sense of reality. The rise of globalisation has brought about the destruction of numerous natural indigenous cultures and introduced new ones based on material ethics.

It becomes clear that real self-consciousness can only be achieved through a better understanding of human and environmental realities. This simple yet honest approach to the way we perceive the world and each other will lead to an infinitely more accurate understanding of knowledge and life that can assist in the selective re-introduction of natural cultures and values more reflective of the human condition. This focus on a more natural human development in all elements of society will lead to self-realisation giving people a truer sense of identity and a greater purpose for living their lives.

These are the main issues worth considering in relation to the past, present and future of African peoples and their descendants:

1. Redemption may well be past its sell-by date as the wages of sin have well and truly been paid in full.

2. Reparations could not possibly begin to atone for one life let alone the countless millions that suffered and died for wretched worldly gains.
3. Repatriation can hardly be appealing for many descendants of Africa whose original native homeland continues to be gang-raped of its resources and kept with no soul.

Sadly there are many other issues needing to be addressed. An inheritance of the material and metaphysical follies of the world should not be an option in, anyway. The three points raised need not be so pessimistically cynical, however. The truth will always out and is always stranger than fiction.

PHILIP MORGAN was born in London in 1965 and has demonstrated his interests and concerns for the socially disadvantaged by working with several organisations and charities as a volunteer. Having pledged a lifelong commitment to genuine good causes, he is a positive advocate of good all round health focusing on physical, personal and spiritual health aspects in particular. His work with THACMHO has gone from strength to strength as this book, in part, will testify.

The White Raven Tavern

THACMHO BLACK HISTORY COMMITTEE HOLDS ITS MEETINGS on the original site of the White Raven Tavern. This was a substantial inn built just outside the Parish of Whitechapel. It provided overnight accommodation for visitors, had its own stables, served food and drink and provided space for local meetings. Frequently it was the place chosen for inquests, being close to London Hospital. George Hannay, a prominent doctor on the Board of the London Hospital probably suggested the venue when he became involved in the Committee for the Relief of the Black Poor. Hannay played a significant role in getting the project off the ground, and two places were chosen where weekly sums were doled out to London's Black poor. The other was at the Yorkshire Stingo, in Lissom Green near Marylebone.

The discovery of old brickwork in the basement of the Whitechapel Mission raised the question as to whether this was part of the structure of the old tavern, and perhaps the level of the road had subsequently risen. We hope further research can answer this question.

Photography (below) taken in the basement of the Whitechapel Mission, 212 Whitechapel Road. Our research has indicated that this is the most likely site of the White Raven Tavern, where the Committee for the Relief of the Black Poor paid their allowances. The tradition of helping the poorest in the community has continued to date by the Whitechapel Mission who do important work with the homeless. (see www.whitechapel.org.uk)

Eighteenth century wall exposed during excavations at the Whitechapel Mission in 2002

Books by the Power Writers

Phillis Wheatley
Poems on Various Subjects Religious and Moral, Archibald Bell, London (1773).

Ukawsaw Gronniosaw
A Narrative of the Most Remarkable Particulars In the Life of James Albert Ukawsaw Gronniosaw, An African Prince, As related by Himself, Gye and Mills, Bath (1772).

John Marrant
A Narrative of the Lord's Wonderful Dealings with John Marrant, a black, now going to preach the Gospel in Nova Scotia, self-published (1785).

A Sermon Preached on the 24th day of June 1789, Being the Festival of St John the Baptist, at the request of the Right Worshipful Grand Master Prince Hall, and the Rest of the Brethren of the African Lodge of the Honourable Society of Free and Accepted Masons in Boston, by the Reverend Brother Marrant, Chaplain, Boston (1789).

A Journal of the Rev. John Marrant from August 1785 to the 16th March 1790, London (1790).

Olaudah Equiano
The Interesting Narrative of the Life of Olaudah Equiano or Gustavus Vassa the African, self-published, London (1789).

Quobna Ottobah Cugoano
Thoughts and Sentiments on the Evil and Wicked Traffic on the Commerce of the Human Species, self-published, London (1787). This includes 'The Narrative of the Enslavement of Ottobah Cugoano a Native of Africa' as an appendix.

Further Reading

Unchained Voices: An Anthology of Black Authors in the English-Speaking World of the 18th Century, edited by Vincent Carretta, University Press of Kentucky, Lexington (1996). This book deals with all our Power Writers.

Black England: Life Before Emancipation, Gretchen Gerzina, Allison & Busby, London (1999).

Black Poor and White Philanthropists: London's Blacks and the Foundation of the Sierra Leone Settlement 1786-1791, Stephen Braidwood, Liverpool University Press, Liverpool (1994).

Black Settlers in Britain 1555-1958, Nigel File and Chris Power, Heinemann Educational Books, London (1981).

The History of Lion Walk Congregational Church, E.A. Blaxill, Colchester (1939).

I was Born a Slave: An Anthology of Classic Slave Narratives, edited by Yuval Taylor, Payback Press, Edinburgh (1999).

The Many-Headed Hydra, The Hidden History of the Revolutionary Atlantic, Peter Linebaugh and Marcus Rediker, Verso, London and New York (2000).

Our Children Happy and Free: Letters from Black Settlers in Africa in the 1790s, Christopher Fyfe (ed.), Edinburgh University Press, Edinburgh (1991).

Pan-Africanism for Beginners, Sid Lemelle, Writers and Readers, New York and London (1992).

Staying Power: The History of Black People in Britain, Peter Fryer, Pluto Press, London (1984).

The Axe Laid to the Root: The Story of Robert Wedderburn, Martin Hoyles, Hansib Publications, London (2004).

APPENDIX

Utilising the Power Writers Walking Tour

Caribbean African Students Project in conjunction with Ethnic Minority Achievement Service

CELEBRATING BLACK HISTORY MONTH IN SCHOOLS

This book was used as a component for a photographic project involving six Tower Hamlets schools.

The aim of the project was to raise the awareness of the contribution Africans have made to developing communities. This would be achieved by supporting pupils to identify images they feel represent aspects of Africa in everyday life and objects. These images would be captured in film and a short extract describing the reasoning behind the images. The project was divided into three parts fashion, social documentary and arts and culture.

Under the heading of social documentary, the pupils were invited to attend three after school sessions to learn how to use a single lens reflex (SLR) camera and to look at the five writers identified in the booklet. The pupils were encouraged to research the writers to discover any additional information relevant to the project. On the fourth session, the pupils were given the SLR cameras and were taken on the Power Writers Walking Tour as illustrated in the book.

CONCLUSION

The book was not only very informative but also easy to use and adapt to meet the project's objectives. The layout and content made the information accessible to all pupils irrespective of their academic abilities. The walk was simple to follow and created some good discussion points between the teaching staff and pupils. The only criticism was the buildings and landmarks mentioned in the booklet were not easily identifiable. Many of the structures had changed or were no longer significant.

I have given two copies of the booklet to the library service with a view to incorporating the walk into the history unit of the National Curriculum document.

Ms Adisa Ekundayo